SKUNK CABBAGE

Mudfish Individual Poet Series #4

SKUNK CABBAGE

Poems by
Harry Waitzman

BOX TURTLE PRESS/ATTITUDE ART, INC.
184 FRANKLIN STREET, NEW YORK, NEW YORK 10013

Distributed by: Bernhard DeBoer, 113 East Centre Street, Nutley, NJ 07110 and Ubiquity Distributors, Inc. 607 Degraw St., Brooklyn, NY 11217. Available also from Box Turtle Press.

Jacket Design: Robert Steward and Kit McCracken

Typeset in Futura Book.

Copyright 2004 Box Turtle Press
184 Franklin Street
New York, New York 10013
212.219.9278; mudfishmag@aol.com

ACKNOWLEDGEMENTS

"Tribeca," "Just Birds," *The Seattle Review*

"Ed Hopper in Rockland," "On a November Morning," *Sarah Lawrence Review*

"Anjou Pear," *Abiko Journal*

"Cracks," "Green Island," "I Owe You, Marc Chagall," "Gravity," "Brambles," "Rejected," *Mudfish*

"Aliases," (Henry Lee) *Slipstream*

"The Celestial Kingdom," *Oberon*

"Dirty Pictures," *Inkwell*

for my wife Marcia
and L.L., J.H. and T.L.

CONTENTS

Your thighs are appletrees
whose blossoms touch the sky.

William Carlos Williams

GREEN ISLAND

A cascade of pine
and the trilling of horniness
in my veins. Clouds billow

and blot chimneys. I pinch
my wife's bottom in a dream.

The tingling scent of evergreens
spikes my cheeks.

We pick fights like berries
and make up. Her tongue clasps
mine. Her hips bruise gently.

Birds fly in from exotic islands
carrying proof and offerings.
I approach this green land

circled by a granite necklace
polished by sun and wave lap.

ANJOU PEAR

My anjou pear blushes when I pinch
her bottom in public. I'm careful
curators at galleries don't notice
how I seek out the shadows, places
where the bulbs have burned out,
stair landings where you feel
for the bottom step with your toe.
In all these places, I check for ripeness.

ED HOPPER IN ROCKLAND

A while ago, before my grey hair and grandchildren,
Ed Hopper drove up from his home in Nyack
and painted the Mobilgas station in Valley Cottage
on Route 303 before it was widened.

The picture drops stones down an empty well
but you can hear splashes if you lean forward and listen.
The three gas pumps stand as caryatids supporting
a temple of progress. I hear a Mack truck loaded

with gravel grinding up the hill. The two lane highway
runs everywhere and nowhere; the future peels clouds
stuck to the sky. His brush paints the Victorian house
by the railroad. Hopper's Dodge picks me up

and we roll on to the Automat. America separates
husbands and wives, friends and lovers.
A woman in the sun poses alone in her room
without clothes. I crawl in through the open window.

POSTCARD FROM PARIS

The color of your voice is honey,
your accent, dashes of salt and pepper.
You swim in the pool every morning,
your hair is damp when we meet.

When you are away, my head rolls
in Chinatown, like a garbage can cover.
I hang out below the curbs of Mulberry
Street where a blue dragon corners me.

I become a monk for four weeks
taking a vow of unhappiness.
Until you return from visiting your
parents, you promise to become a nun
enjoined to piety.

Your last postcard says nothing except
you are alive and it's dangerous for me
to write to you.

GRAVITY

Headless, hunkered down, a few ducks bob in a circle
as I drive by the reservoir in the rain.
I'm comfortable in my car, heater on, wipers clearing
the view of raindrops thickening the windshield.

I'm driving home to four walls and an argument.
Yesterday I dropped a coffee cup on my wife's toe.
Married for over forty years, one doesn't throw things,
but lets gravity do the trick.

THE CELESTIAL KINGDOM

hides behind the Great Wall of China straddling
Bowery and Canal Street. I enter like a rat in daylight
slipping through a crack in the masonry. Chinese fish
stores stand guard next to green grocers offering
Shanghai rabe and other exotic vegetables.

Smells of heaven and fish imprint the crowded streets.
On Bayard, fat dakon and winter melon sell for pennies.
I walk to the nearest fish store. The fishmonger eyes me
as I ask for striped bass. He points to a sea trout. I slip inside,
find a large bass and lift the gills. He laughs as if

to ask where "round eyes" learned to check if fish was fresh.
I'm still my father's son and he was a fishman. I put my hands
in the ice to clean them. The chips are soothing gems,
slippery, cool. They calm me and I'm young again.
I yell, "that one," pointing to a beauty. He almost bows

weighing it. It is half the cost of sea bass at the A&P.
I yell, "head off, fillet it with bone on and double bag it."
He puts the knife down, read to crook his bloody arm around
my shoulders. He's my friend now and I'm in a good mood.
I rush off with my package to keep my appointment.

Time stops for me every Wednesday at one o'clock.
I meet my friend under the shadows of the steel scaffolding
at the corner of Bayard and Mulberry. I greet her,
she brushes my cheeks with her lips and electrifies my afternoon.

SHMUTZ

I have known the incandescence of noon
strolling in the shmutz of Manhattan.
Now the leaves of spring are withering,
the azalias brightening brownstone streets
fling their flowers and fade. I walk
alone, cloud weight on my shoulders, bark
on my tongue.

I backed into middle age and older,
eyes shut and no wiser, but in the backing,
so much, so much — everything.

BRAMBLES

The blackberry canes spring up
between pebbles and sand along
the gravel road leading to Parker Pond.

Notice how small the berries are
this year. There must have been a shortage
of rain in spring. July's been an oven.

I worry about my wife, more bossy
and anxious under her hair coloring.
We snap at each other like turtles.

Kicking stones, I come to a weathered
glacial boulder shaded by a stand of white pine
—I must fall in love with my wife again.

THE COW ON MY DOORSTEP

Once I tried to grab the tail of a cow
and got swatted on my face.
I was alone with the smell of hay
in the barn and the sound of swallows
whirring in the eaves.

I tried milking the young Guernsey
and got blisters on my fingers.
After bandaging them, I tried again
and missed the pail more often than not.
In a month I made music on the metal.

CHINESE APPLES

I brace myself on the bow
of the ferry to Manhattan
and brush the squawks
of seagulls from my overcoat.
I stamp my feet; occasional
glints of sunshine escape
from clouds and warm my face.
My expectations rise with the Hudson's
flood tide and churn violently
as the ship backs into its berth.

The walls of her apartment
are clothed in silk, she rustles
in her gown and brings me
tea and kumquats. I kiss her
lips and taste ripe pomegranates,
the red juice runs down my chin,
a month of sunsets burns ahead.
We become matches when we touch
and must find a place to cool off.

We explore the garden behind
St. Lukes Church and rub cheeks.
I imagine I'm a polar bear and she,
a penguin. We scamper on ice floes
and frolic as the ice freezes.
Even a short summer of loving
has the power to melt glaciers.
I bring her a gift of a mackerel,
she pinches her greying lover.

THURSDAY'S SHOES

Papa loved Thom McAn shoes
so much, he bought seven pairs
at a time, carried them home and laid
them out on the dining room table
for all to admire, shining black and brown,
no scuff marks, tongues hanging out clean,
no stinky foot smell, soles unmarked.

His mother had seven children in Poland
and one pair of shoes. Each child wore shoes
one day a week. Papa said he always had
Thursday's shoes. He left his village for America
where the smell of leather inspired fantasies.
He would wear shoes at all hours
of the day and every day of the week.

ON A NOVEMBER MORNING

he slumps at the luncheonette counter,
eyes shut, hearing only eggs fry in bacon fat,
inhaling curls of smoke wisping his way.

In the evening, he orders fish from the short
order cook, no sense gabbing with the fat waitress
who says she's thirty and only a size twelve.

He tells the regulars we are all orphans,
even those with kids and grandchildren. Friends
at the counter are closer than cousins, and the chef's

his father, more giving than his was. Big Mama
on the early shift always gives him a hug and kiss
before perspiration sours her body.

With salt and pepper shakers, he plays a game of chess,
moving knights and pawns. After losing, he reads the Times
and says the world's fucked up, wishing he were on Mars.

He wonders where it will end, stopped smoking
twenty years ago. He keeps stopping—eggs, red meat,
looks at shiksas, these cause palpitations but what

is life without palpitations, a juicy steak, chocolate
melting on your tongue, the tingling in your pants
when a salesgirl smiles and seems to care.

HURRICANE ESTHER

Esther from the fish store clopped
live chicken carp with a wooden clopper,
tossing bloody heads into a weighing
pan while she smiled at customers.

Esther fell near Five Corners, her ankle
swelled but her stepmother said, soak it.

Esther, the fish lady, loved my father,
but he courted Elke, her younger sister
who had an olive complexion and jet
black hair which flew in the rain.

After Elke's wedding, Esther lurched by
train into the arms of relatives in Boston.
She learned to bake beans and grill waffles
and met a tailor who smoked stubby cigars.

*

The break never set right, the leg grew
shorter and bent. She limped slowly so as not
to be noticed and cursed her father's second
wife so busy raising more children.

*

I visit Tante Esther in a nursing home for the first time
in three years. She looks at me as if I'm from Siberia,
then laughs and hugs me. We talk. In minutes
I'm not sixty but six years old, asking for waffles.

She slips back into the kitchen of her walk-up

apartment, the eye of the hurricane, protection
against gusts from my wounding parents. On
an old waffle iron she pours batter that grills brown.

At ninety-four, she keeps me feeling young
and talks about her son and my mother, her beautiful
sister, "all gone."

I walk to the parking lot, tasting a distant sweetness
on my tongue, my stomach aching but full.

HALF-SOUR ON THE EAST SIDE

I've been soaked in a pickle barrel
that squats on an Orchard Street sidewalk,
hoops and staves curved around my head.
I emerge with bumps, dripping brine,
tongue running across the roof of my mouth
as I spit out cloves and pickling spices.

The color of my skin is monster green.
Dogs walk around me and sniff. They
bark, but none try to bite.
I wear a sprig of dill as an ornament
as if I were a knight with a plume
charging to Ratner's on Delancey Street.

I order platters of matjes herring with onions,
and pumpernickel with black tea in a glass.
This may be my last meal before time executes me,
or I jump from the Williamsburg Bridge.
One last piece of prune Danish and I'd go happy.
A little strudel wouldn't be bad either.
And seltzer, please more seltzer.

ON MY 61ST BIRTHDAY

I scratch for images, like the chicken
fifty years rotted
and still clucking in my head.

Invisible radio waves carry Hitler's voice
into the kitchen from Vienna. His speech
detonates "Seig Heils."

Our German shepherd paces, tantalyzed
by fat hens. The bitch rips steel
and leaps into red feathers.

Fifty years of sleep dilute my grief. Yellow
chicken feet float in a soup of memory,
steaming, flecked with parsley.

I bait each dawn with worms on a fishhook
and tug at the sleeve of the world.
The embraceable future begins with love.

BELOW PIERMONT

Winter fog chews the top of Hook Mountain.
Grey ghosts ride waves piling into the Palisades.
Life at the flood of middle age is a backward glance,
a celebration of simple acts of flotation.

Every tide salts the taste of this river,
renewing Piermont's marshes. Drops of rain
transfuse parched wetlands harboring eagles
and ospreys.

The river eddies in solitude frothed with bird cries.
I move forward, gills half gone, tail appending
a half inch to my skeleton.

BRAHMS

I hold your hand at the concert
even though you are away in Paris.
We forget small gestures

when love progresses to a hot shower
and coming in your bedroom.
I watch the pianist leap into the piano.

During the Brahms First,
I sway back and forth and touch you,
my eyes following the conductor's baton.

Can I follow you
to your mother's apartment near St. Germain?
Her arm is broken but she still hugs you.

I hope she liked her gifts, especially
the blue foot warmers I bought her.
Were they warm and the right size?

I walk through descending chords, listening
to melodies of loneliness. Darkness hurts. I hear
your voice reverberate, like a distant kettle drum.

THE FALCONER

In the first days of spring, I lose my winter
shadow and walk alone, the sun perched
on my shoulder. Yellow light floods
morning.

I rub azalia buds as if they were nipples
and reach for magnolia blossoms curled
tight against the last snow.

THE MATZOH FACTORY

Let the aperture of my 35 mm. camera focus
on the grimy factory, "Streit's Matzoh since 1928,"
one year after I was born. My eyes squint and see
through the brick walls. Stripped to their pupiks,
men feed dough into hungry ovens.

Take one bucket of water from the East River,
mix with three shovels of dirt from the corner
of Rivington and Suffolk Streets, add a handful
of salt without yeast and bake on the sidewalk
for the desired square shape.

Bless this bread of affliction for the Jews, bless
these wafers for the Catholics, bless this white bread
for the Protestants, plain or toasted. Father, I need
bread, loaves of affection, even crumbs will do,
with seeds and cuttings to reforest the desert.

The Pharaoh laughs, "I'll let them bake
to contentment and snuff out their lives, unleavened
bread will stick in their throats. My chariots will
race over the River, up Delancey Streeet and turn
on Rivington. The insurgents holed up in Streit's

will fly to heaven on flames from an ancient oven."

KISS

I always squeak in the morning
until the sun rises to warm my bones.
I take false steps and half breaths.
My surgeon says,
two lower vertebrae kiss
and cause the spasms in my back.

I take the latest pain killers,
and worry about my kidneys.
What a tradeoff—bending from the waist,
or losing my ability to piss.
I tiptoe past a coffin,

don't like the color of the satin.
The dead man wears a silk jock strap.
I live between the bones of my body.

JAPANESE BLOCK PRINT

The waitress jiggles her tray, bows
and serves the main course.
A smile is frozen on her face. I admire
her body, slim as a robin's.

The manager of the Hakone Hotel picks well.
I wish I were a hawk. She is beautiful
in a strange distant way. I've seen her
before, but where?

Impossible. Her oval face balances above
her shoulder's thin frame. But the legs
dismay me. She is bowlegged as all Japanese
girls seem to be.

She comes closer and smiles, aware
that I'm staring at her. Hai!
Yes, I know her, in a block print by Utamaro,
probably her great, great grandmother.

BELOVED THIS, BELOVED THAT

A putty landscape spreads out before me.
When the body arrives a whistling embalmer
draws one eyebrow longer than the other.
The cadaver is rouged and laid out for the wake.

On Old Mill Road the pastures are untouched
by cow's tongues for half a century. Foundations
of pegged chestnut barns rise out of the water.
I smell horse manure steaming in the morning.
Veneers of time peel away.

At the cemetery, I kneel before the open
casket as relatives gather. The minister praises
the deceased and twists the facts. In the satin of
a coffin, gruffness is trapped. Worn by rain and ice,
names on a tombstone wash away. Headstones
announce less caring and more connections,
"Beloved this, Beloved that."

As I drive home, my world turns upside down.
I sing like a cicada to my love.
My shrill voice resounds off the ceiling
of her bathroom as I shower and dry off.

At night my hands remember pockets of hunger
and move along familiar bones. After sex,
we tug at a blanket until subdued by sleep.

LONG POND

A crowd of pines convenes above
Long Pond. Unruly limbs and branches clap.
Bass wake up.

Morning sunlight reddens my ass as I race
naked in the woods and pause at the pond's
edge, searching for loons. A fish hawk

spots my featherless shape trying to fly while
jogging. The bird squeezes between clouds
and unravels silk air skimming over meadows.
I'm jealous of two hikers wrestling in tall grass.
If my wife's hips were wings, we'd soar

and hump on a pillow of clouds plumped
above Fisherman's Island.

MULBERRY STREET

I step down Mulberry Street with you
on my right and the sun overhead.
We are so discreet — no holding hands —
when we stop at the Vietnamese store
where fish bark and vegetables sing.
Although the weather is clear, I feel

blasts from Hatteras and black clouds
block my sight. I walk into the eye of
a hurricane when I take your hand
and touch your shoulder and look above
your head in a storm, our love
like a silk umbrella, wide and handsome.

SWIMMING IN A POLISH RIVER

There is no art to a life lived miserably,
no sympathy either, only regrets, anger.
She died in a transient hotel, the sign,
Hotel on the Square flashing periodically
as if the bulbs had no strength to stay lit.

Her sledgehammer coronary shook
the springs as she collapsed into her bed
without a scream and lay there until
the cleaning lady opened the door
and smelled death from the gut's release.

When the funeral arrangements were complete,
waiting for the body, I remembered to tell
the undertaker her weight. He ordered
the extra large casket, otherwise she might not fit.
She was dropped by gravediggers into a hole

dug next to Mom's. The coffin tilted and she almost
fell out, ready to have one more argument with members
of the family. A year later, her footstone
cracked. Flies that kept her company
buzzed out of the ground.

Tears were scarce for the holy terror
she was from age three, Prozac, maybe sixty years
sooner, and love from her father, would have helped.

She was named Sonya, for a grandmother deceased
in Poland. The name was spoken with fingers pressed
over the lips in hushed tones. Sonya drowned in the river
near the shtetl of Stepin where young, depressed
mothers went swimming.

THE POISON TREE

I'm overcome by the oleander flowers
in Feng Hu's Buddhist Park. The odor
seems thick as molasses and clogs my throat.
Like a flea, I search for crevices,
cracks, and wooden doors open to breathe.

I take the lift to Devil's Garden where
tourists are asked to burn money and incense.
The Temple's signs (in three languages)
promise wealth and a long life. The fake
money burns too fast, the thin tapers

sting my throat. In the Garden
of Veiled Life, I stoop to touch a butterfly
and pray for a lovely companion. The insect
lingers on a low branch of a twisted pine
shading the courtyard a thousand years.

RUMORS OF MYSELF

I check the stacks at Poet's House and envy the young poets
published in thin volumes with hard covers. Unable to work
in cloistered places, I slip out to the elevator unrecognized.

I stroll along Spring Street alone, there's no romance left,
screwing's become an act of extreme unction that stresses
the heart. I'm not dead yet but write travelogues not poetry,

admonishes Mark Doty. I bump into two well-dressed
women. "Don't I know you?" A drink at a wine bar
and small talk. I inhale blue smoke from Marlene's lips,

Deborah's radiant, still wet from the surf pounding Oahu.
Yes, beauty with a long shelf life. Like Mama with her
olive skin and halo of long tresses, in love with Papa

and Ronald Coleman on Saturdays, her hair looped in an
elegant bun crowning her forehead, her Russian loveliness
unspoiled by hairdressers. I want to drive back

to my childhood along Sunrise Highway, cousins hanging
onto Papa's fish truck as it lurches to Jamaica Bay where
sandwiches were born, where Mama fanned her bosom,

haven for boys bitten by black flies and jellyfish. Life's lived
on a spiral, not simply plunging and rising but edging forward.
Educated by mishaps and screwups, I've bled, enjoying fewer

laughs than cries. I remember the horseshoe crabs thrown
on the beach skittering to hide in seaweed below the shallows
where terns dive to kill. I'm still panic-stricken by the sound

of pebbles clacking as the tide runs out and grabs my ankles.
Mama's gone, my lifeguard against sea monsters and eye-

pecking birds. I walk along Jones Beach searching for shells,

a place to write. Even to this day, I tremble when I see
a herring gull circle over my head, swoop low and open its
yellow beak. I have one chance left to spread rumours of myself.

BULLFINCH

Some mornings I'm dizzy, as if the world
and all its earthworms got up without me.
I toss in bed, shutting out first light.
Rising, I tread water in a hot shower,
my razor and shaving cream, tools
of the dumb beast I've become.
My wife's alarm sounds again
as I pull the tie tighter around my neck.

In a frame on the dining room wall
pressed between glass and matte,
Hokusai's *Bullfinch* sways
on a snow-laden cherry branch.
My stare bends the icy bough
and the bird whirls and darts
round the room in widening arcs,
until a chirping starts within my ear
and clouds dust Mt. Fuji's rim.

Counting the crumbs on my plate,
I peck at my breakfast.

TWILIGHT

Twilight is the best light to see
a clothed woman breathe and lift
her breasts a short distance.

She's a novice playwright and manages
chopsticks boldly, each fishball balanced with
noodles. Juggling careers is the problem.

We hold coffee cups instead of hands.
Our lips kiss the haze of fumes from waiting
cabs. We leave the sidewalk cafe smiling.

On Bayard Street, I'm mugged by anxiety
and foreboding. I start reading my horoscope
and swallow lies inside my fortune cookies.

RANSOM

I suffered a memory loss after
you left and could barely type France
on my word processor. When we
said good-bye, you took my tongue
and it went through customs. I paid

a ransom to free myself, by finally
admitting to strong feelings. In Maine,
I count silver boats slapping water
and the number of Wednesdays
until you return.

TWELVE MIRROR CARP

The carp's head flies from its flapping body.
Papa's blade flashed in a downward arc
cutting through the gills. Blood squirts like water
from a hose. I close my eyes. My head falls
from my body and rolls in the sawdust.

Twelve mirror carp swim in a steel tank.
Without scales, their skin is light green,
translucent, their flesh the pink of roses.
With kicks of dorsal fins, twelve mirrors adjust
to my height. I can barely see the water.

Before sundown, Friday, the tank is drained.
Slimy water gurgles down a rusty pipe, coughs
and plunges into the sewer. Three unsold carp
thrash and blow bubbles, slowly dying out of water.
Papa packs them in ice for sale on Monday.

On *Shabbat* I read prayers about the New Year,
how confession opens Heaven's Gates to sinners.
I poked a fish with my thumb and jabbed five
times with a broom handle until it bled. "Dumb
fish, dumb fish," I yelled.

Monday after school, I'm back to asking
questions of clouds and trees in a loud voice
which upsets Papa. I approach an old maple
whose roots quietly lift the sidewalk,

"Where do mirror carp come from?
Are they heaven's messenger to the poor
who can't afford whitefish and salmon?"

Papa, taller than a tree, dances
out of the fish store, shaking sawdust
from felt boots large as lifeboats.

His bloody apron wraps around his belly
like a red sail. He pats his bulging pockets
stuffed with dollar bills. "Yes," he says,

"because we smack laughter to lips
that mourn, greet good luck with groans
and remember the sweet taste of chicken
carp, the yellow belly a sash of saffron."

SCALLION TALK

Pacing on Bayard waiting for you,
I examine exotic fruits and vegetables
and wish I could speak Chinese. Some fruits
look as if they were grown on the far side
of the moon, some speak to me in a low

voice from Mars saying, "Lucky fellow,
you must have won her in the New York State
Lottery. She's a prize so pinch her gently, she bruises
so easily, like a kumquat."

In Chinatown, I don't argue with luck or fate
and wish the fat winter melon would sit quietly
and mind its own business. His sidekick pipes up
from the counter, "she speaks fluent Mandarin
with a foreign accent but it pleases my Shanghai ear.

"Be impressed by her accomplishments, she sings
in the Beijing Opera and would please
the Emperor." The scallion scowls and wishing me
no harm whispers, "But remember she's young
and in ten years you'll be an old man."

BLACK MIRRORS

Down gutters and leaders
raindrops slide, halting on asphalt
where they polish black mirrors.
I walk face down, smiling at the man

looking up. I'm tired, the years
are seamless from birth to heart attack.
Yet I straighten my posture, throw
my chest out and admire the lilacs asleep
and tulips tunneling up to light.

Soon the bulbs buried in dirt will stir
and greet glum sparrows, dripping
song. My baton touches white clouds
as crows pepper Spring with cackles.

HOT PEPPERS

While you were away in Paris, I went back
to our Vietnamese restaurant. I noticed straw
hats tacked to the walls, the kind farmers
and the V.C. wore into battle. Were they
just nailed up, or did your presence

blind me to everything except your lips
and fingers clicking chopsticks. Today
I drown in hot peppers again but hear
your laugh when my nose turns red.

CRACKS

With you gone, I fall into the cracks
of a sidewalk in Chinatown.
Orange peel, candy wrappers curl
over me. I feel smaller than
a burnt match or the pit of an apple.

STUDIO IN FLORENCE

I lean on a marble pedestal unclothed,
my right leg cramped, the left numb.
After standing for several hours, I reach
for a shot of Grappa. As I pose
for posterity, my crotch begins to itch.

From loins of grass, I weave days
into weeks as young Italians gesticulate.
Happiness is fleeting like ants marching
up their hill. I rest my head on the rubble
of an arch and hear Caesar's legions pass.

I bend over draft stanzas and chisel
away to free a poem. I unclasp the wings
of words as chips fall on my toes. I stand
naked with pubic hairs combed by light,
penis limp and circumcised. I am no David.

I'm the model for no one but myself.
The cast was broken; the mold spilled wax.
No awards beckoned; my voice became hoarse.
I was reduced to a word, or two, in the right order;
from syllables, a sound, from sounds, a life.

CAKES OF ICE

delivered in Pasquale's wagon were like
carrera marble. The blue slabs were chipped
into ice flakes and sprinkled over fish. When
Papa dipped his hands into the ice they were

shovels searching for large yellow pike
and whitefish. He snatched carp from a tank
waving a torn cotton net. I shrank back
to my childhood watching him work.

Bellowing at customers in Yiddish, joking
in greenhorn English, he insulted all
but sold fish cheaper than his competitors.
I was allowed to take cash on holidays

and God forbid if I didn't say thank you
when the customer paid me. I wanted to sell
carp and halibut, clopping the knife like Papa
while strutting on sawdust soaked in blood.

He wouldn't let me. "You're going to be a
doctor-lawyer." I waited, remembering
to look for fins of pike and teeth of eels
writhing in a gunny sack. With both, you

put your hands in a den of razors. Once
on Friday he was swamped and let me sell fillet
from 50 lb. cans resting on ice. I asked to do more.
He was an iron man behind a wooden counter.

So long as ice chips refracted the colors of
the rainbow, Papa was God of light and darkness,
of smiles and wrath. His foreign accent pierced

eardrums, sweat from his brow flooded my nights.

He rooted in red sawdust in America
but wore a Russian cap and boots. Fish
scales like silver coins filled his pants pockets.
He shook himself free of guts and entrails

before going home in the evening to soak
his punctured fingers. Mama checked cuts,
boiled water and added strong disinfectants.
Black ichthammol salve stopped infections.

I learned in the slime and blood where
life came from and how it was sustained
by the roe and milt of creatures with
barbs and gills. We are all related.

The odor from the store whistled past kerchiefs,
the wooden floor sagged and squeaked,
tired of holding the weight of boxes
and Bubbas with pennies in their purses.

Today, I go through life with dry hands,
afraid of this, afraid of that.
When he caught me his eyes relented,
but he wouldn't hand me a knife.

CHAMPAGNE

My love was wearing nothing
but a champagne glass
when I snapped the picture.
The wine fizzed, the cork popped
and discretion flew through the air.

HOMAGE TO MARINA TSVETAYEVA

Sharks swim across Red Square and eat the street
lamps. One star pries open the darkness. Marina,

just married, was molten, her young body magma.
She was a new icon in the salons and wrote poems

that cracked like Cossack whips. When she walked hand
in hand with Mandelstam, their heartbeats shook

the establishment. Ossip and Marina, a pair of lovers
waltzing across the slippery floors of Moscow.

The audacity to praise Germans after Tannenberg!
What mania for revolver clicks drove Ossip

to describe Stalin as possessing ten worn fingers
and a cockroach mustache?

What spirit intoxicated Russian poets to write
for grandchildren while digging their graves with a pen?

She rinsed common sense from her hair and walked
out of her toilette, poet of tomorrow, above cabals

and convention, true to her glottic voice.
She blunted reality by hanging herself.

She lies in a grave marked only by swirling leaves.
Snow flakes, grass in season, guard her skull and bones.

Here's a toast, not to a new dawn but to rusty sunsets.
Prosit Marina! A little herring on black bread has its place.

CHINESE FUNERAL

Night falls like a hammer and my dreams
are glass. I walk down Doyers Street alone,
ghosts ride on my shoulders: my wife
and children. The pavement crumbles, shuttered
stores surround me. I bang into a hydrant.

Men and women file past me like automatons.
The crowd thins to cardboard. A black shape,
a hearse with its rear door open, limos parked
on Mulberry. I look at a faded sign in script,
"Ng Fook Funerals." The family gathers

for a last moment of prayer, buoyed by flowers
and incense. So young but filled with death.
She sleeps nearby in an apartment filled with books.
I call from a phone booth on the street. Her husband's
away but he rides behind me in the elevator.

CLOUD BURSTS

Rain rolls off my forehead and blurs
my vision. I forget my hat and umbrella
and sometimes forget my wife.

Pop-eyed pansies flutter near the ground,
flirting with irises, winking at children
making mud pies.

I open my arms to ink-stained rain
dripping from the eaves of the library.
My book of thoughts is dirty.

I watch a yellow-blue pansy
kiss the foot of a towering brown iris,
my violets shrink from contact.

Can there be love between curved blades
of grass lying on each other in a field?
Thistles elope hitched on stockings.

Nature mimics man, a bull frog hops
to his female, mates grumpily, with no thanks
or foreplay and leaves.

I admire the attraction between spiders,
the black widow swoops down on her love
and kisses him until he is dead.

I OWE YOU, MARC CHAGALL

In Chinatown I sip oolong tea incognito
after choking on rice and black beans
spiced with red peppers from Viet Nam.

The Chinese elders chatting on park benches
know time is as wrinkled as their faces. Darkness
and light fall on withered grass with equal weight.

Many old-timers smile through the spaces
in their mouths where molars were extracted
by the Bayard Street shoemaker.

Legs crossed on the sidewalk, he pulled nails
from worn shoes and teeth from infected jawbones.
The poor waited on line patiently for his pliers.

These scenes are time and a continent away
from Vitebsk, tied together by worn shoelaces
and tears glued on leathery Jewish cheeks.

Still when I walk through the Jewish Museum
showing your paintings, a woman slips from
a gold frame and kisses me full on the lips.

My wife won't mind, it happened in my imagination.
Maybe I'm married forty years in my head.
When poor, I ate a herring with a potato every day.

JUST BIRDS

The birds, a pair, stretch their long necks
and shovel their orange bills into the lake.
You know what they are called.
They move their mouths and swivel
their necks to reach tender plants.
Feathers stained brown or streaked yellow,
they can be untidy, dropping feathers
along the shore. I find one quill,
unbroken, flaring white almost incandescent
in my hand. I imagine the peaks flown over,
the driving beat of four wings.
I'm separated from my friend.

THE WHITE CRANE

A swoop over my shoulder and bounce,
then the lightest thud of white as red eyes
part bullrushes in search of darting fish.

I hold my breath fearing the bird will fly
away leaving me alone. I applaud its circus legs,
strutting across the silk fog and blue sky,

unrolling on a Chinese scroll. With his mate,
they celebrate bonding for almost eighty years.
They will scratch and cackle in Soho's

Guggenheim another week. Then fly
to a larger pond in the Capital where their plumed
feathers will surprise visitors. I envy their

staying power. Mine is short — my skinny neck
won't stretch the length of a wooden hoe.

CLIMBING THE GREAT WALL

My Irma flies to Beijing and rides her bike
into the countryside bumping her French behind
on Chinese stones. Collecting songs of straw in villages,
she records on her Sony the panoply of falsetto reviving
classic opera in cities. In a hotel for students, my bluebird
sings after midnight and undresses by a naked bulb.

My wife and I vacation cheaply in Edgewater
at the Hero Han Restaurant. She eats salmon and tuna
shushi and purrs. I order Udon noodles which steam
and wiggle in the bowl. I chase them with chopsticks
and slurp them down. The Hudson gleams, a witness to
a prior rendezvous. I become dizzy.

Children shout and race around the tile pool
near the stair landing. They frighten four green turtles
which paddle wildly to get away. I tell them, "Be gentle
with the turtles, they might be your deceased uncles
and aunts." I know what I say isn't true,
but lie a little to survive.

ALIASES

I disguise my feelings, wear a broad brimmed
hat and avoid eye contact. My cigar makes
smoke so my profile is obscured. I look
behind, over padded shoulders, and three
decades go by. Cadillacs idle their engines
impatiently at a funeral on Mulberry Street.

With cops all over leaning on kids, I avoid
committing minor offenses. I hold back spitting
in the subway and slip quarters into the meters.
For luck the "Nam" veteran with black glasses
gets a fiver. He won't finger me. Love is dead,
murdered. I did it with premeditation. Desire

still bursts through my brain like a diver
rising after the plunge from the high board.
Every block I get closer to Chinatown makes
her attraction stronger. I'm stuck like a fly
on yellow stickum twisting from the ceiling
of a noodle shop. In the distance, I see a rickshaw
that will take me to my love.

THE LAKE

No wind, the clouds are glued to the sky
and the lake reaches up to steal reflections
from the shore. A glacier streaked boulder

sits on the bank, half in, half out of water.
I wonder which world is real?
Water slaps stone, wings spank air.

My world has dimpled kneecaps.
She moves in a balanced orbit
through underbrush towards the boats.

I ask her to walk along the shore,
and marvel at the polished images of her
neck and breasts. I kiss her twice.

THE MODESTY OF WEEDS

The weeds will flower by late August
and I will celebrate thistles and goldenrod,
and more if I remember their names.

My flesh is flesh of tubers pushing
down into dirt to hide from a *Deere* mower.
My lips have the color of sumac, bright red

when crushed, poisonous when kissed.
I grieve for my *rex begonias* dead by hailstorm
as I drive to the Nanuet Free Library.

I read an article in Harper's Magazine
that America has become as imperial as Rome.
I dream gladiators cut the lawns of America.

Mr. Scheu closed down his greenhouses
because roses were flown in from Columbia.
He keeps rakes and shears handy.

Around me is the modesty of weeds,
the green leaves spring from strong stems
and know their place and beauty.

DELANCEY AND ORCHARD

My father flees to this wide country carrying
rat traps and leading a cow. Immigration
officers give the cow an Irish name. It passes
the physical but still can't spell. Mother
greases a frying pan with *schmaltz*
and makes a banquet of bones.

Father buys a pushcart, a movable department
store, and sells shoelaces and garters,
pots and pans. Kleins on the Square, he's not.
Cobblestones are swept by the skirts of girls
bargaining for braids of licorice. A prostitute
paces Second Avenue holding a broken doll.

Delancey is a sea of hands, waving, poking
cabbage, an island of Yiddishkeit. Mothers descend
like crows cawing strange languages, wings protecting
their young. Black-hat Hasidim rub shoulders
with hoarse socialists, both hunker down in Tompkin's
Square and cry for relief from death's repetitions.

Growing up under a canopy of clouds, we yell
from fire escapes and drop bags of water
on gangs crossing the street. The cow won't
climb the iron stairs and says she wants to return
to Russia, the grass is greener in Minsk.
Every morning the sun comes and sits on our laps.

YELLOW POEM HARBORING FLEAS

1.
Look for a stray banana.
One that barks quietly
and jumps through hoops
and chases children,

a clown really,
who faces pain with growls,
clasps and rides a horse backwards
and pees in the ear of an elephant,

who sleeps inside the Big Top
and lives his life without a safety net,
snoring like the giant gorilla
caged in the corner of my eye.

2.
O gaudiness and sawdust,
and flashy Queens with big boobs
who strip and lift the tent of your pants
while you turn purple.

O sphincters and orifices,
opening to delights of the flesh
beyond conversation and conventions,
seamy light of another world of senses.

O peanut shells and popcorn,
this dog biscuit life *sputters* into palsy
too soon, with few erections and caresses,

the dead remember only yawns of night.

O vulgarity, salty and pungent,
like *Gold's* horseradish that burns
the throat and eyes, confirming
you're alive though crying.

3.
I hear whines and barks
and a banana trots out of the jungle.
It leaps and chews my earlobes;
the paws and tongue tickle.

I fall in love with this mottled beauty,
smooth-skinned and perfumed. I bite,
nipping soft creamy flesh so easy
to swallow.

I dream a bunch of bananas falls
at my feet. I sniff for happiness
in garbage cans. My life wags,
I scratch for fleas until noon.

MRS. ABELSON'S BUNGALOWS

Mother makes borscht out of sour grass
I help pick. The arrow-shaped leaves
swish in the pot with a cook's incantations
and salt and pepper.

Women spill out of the "kuch alein"
speaking Yiddish, smiles sweeping
paths to sleeping grandchildren.
The sun is watched. *Shabbat* is coming.

I don't understand Yiddish, half the meaning
is in the tears, the rest in the wringing of hands.
I hate the chatter of yentas in Mrs. Abelson's
Bungalow Colony, are they telling

mother I've got a girl friend?
I slide invisibly to the grape arbor
for a peek at the bra flapping
on the clothesline. How do you unhook

the clasp in the back?

TRIBECA

Cloves make me cry.
The cast iron loft buildings lean their roofs
on each other, not one stands alone. I'm reminded
of my age and loneliness.

I peer into the future, a brick wall encloses a brick wall,
mortar washes out every rainfall, making space for a fly's
hurried life, an alley cat's spring to dinner.

I live on the edge without wings or parachute,
sharing a ledge pigeon-wide paved with droppings.
Sparrows spin nests in trees with wire and twigs.

Pocketing my thoughts, paying my way with plastic,
I return to Rockland crusted with grime and sweat.
Hoard your complaints, love freely, I tell myself,
death collects every penny of your life.

STENTS IN MY HEART

Love is four arms and legs thrashing
in darkness. I trip over a Hundu goddess
carved from limestone with four bent elbows.
She dances the prayer of stone for a long life.

I sleep on Bengali streets with dried
cow dung my pillow. I waste away to skin
and bones, my toenails grow inward. Dandruff
falls from sparse hairs, one flake at a time.

My scalp hangs loose on my skull.
I think I could take it off like a cap
if I tried. I feel so Irish saying this,
my tongue twists in a whiskey glass.

What has this got to do with love?
I'm falling apart at the groin, that's what,
one arm pit gathers moss when I disrobe,
the other provides a nest for wrens.

My eyes lead me to temptation in the valley
of clits but my body won't follow.
I crave the fair winds from Kashmir. Millet
spills from my mouth. Cobras play in my ear.

Following the path of a working elephant,
I swim in a holy river filled with crocodiles.
I'm an amputee with two arms and legs
and private parts which sometimes

rest in storage. If you carve a vulva
from limestone, my cock stiffens.
I have an itch to scratch a body, not anybody,

but Shiva, goddess of love with three heads.

I chew on six hard teats, heavenly candy,
and plug four orifices. Such holiness!
After chest pains, a magician implants
stents in my heart. I dive for black pearls

in the moon's opaline seas. I grab
the wings of a great white swan
and hijack its flight plan, soaring above
the lakes and homes of Congers.

My feathers though frayed, beat hard enough.

WALKING TO AMERICA

Father told me rain fell upside down
on his village when he was a boy
and he walked on the whiskers of wolves
to Warsaw when he was ten.

Poland grew corpses like potatoes.
Vodka of the peasants ran over 100 proof.
Priests swayed in high pulpits; the foxes
of Krakow romped in chicken coops.

Father pulled up his pants at fourteen,
folded a kerchief around black bread
and a herring and started walking.
The Atlantic was a puddle.

CORDUROY YEARS

She stooped and plucked
a daisy spreading tiny wings
and placed it in the buttonhole
of my worn corduroy jacket.

How neat the yellow against brown cloth,
her smile against my continuous scowl,
my age against hers,
the future of furtive love against present joy.

CHOP CHOP

I use a can opener, the electric kind,
to open the roof of the house
and the building spins and flips.
I shake the people out small as peas,
green as beans,
my eyes, like razors,
       go chop, chop and slit
the air
and heads slide into the frying pan
with browned onions.

In my father's house the carpets were worn,
the attic was cluttered with 78 r.p.m. records,
Harry James, best of the lot and Bruno Walter
conducting the Coriolanus Overture.
The master bedroom bulged from fights,
forty years were packed in a wet basement,
       each coloring the other,
a collage bleeding memories and slowly
peeling the wallpaper away.

KAFKA'S HINGES

The stones of Prague were his prison;
he lived between the street lamps
and gutters leading to the Charles Bridge.
His pen and notebook, his confidante,
his stories were doors clanging open
and shut on hinges of pain. The indescribable
was described by a clerk who heard
insects scurry in kitchens of the capital.

His voice was a current wide as the Moldau,
kissed by soft-mouthed carp, a fisher of hallucinations.
Though his mind flew on bat's wings and dissolved
in mauve and yellow devil's smoke, his body
remained on probation.

We are all smashed stones and rubble,
rain washes over us, horses piss on us,
carriages roll over us, we are stateless
without passports, denied work permits,
our minds and beliefs in straitjackets,
carrying the world and a cockroach on our backs.

REJECTED

My poem is a dead horse
that attracts flies and stinks
to the end of town.
My friends avoid it, wishing
it had been shot and staggered
to its death elsewhere.
A child walks close to the tail
and pulls. Horsehair comes out
of the carcass in long strands.
The boy yells and does an Indian
war dance around the body.
The horse winks.

MELON FROM MAROC

In an hour we depart from the Garde Norte
to visit Renoir's lily gardens.
We leave a melon from Maroc in our apartment.
Yesterday when pinched it was rock-hard.
I detected the smell of Moroccan fields
weeded by unwashed children. I hear
thunder roll off the Atlas Mountains.
I'm not sure if the smell of dung
is from camels or the family donkey.

I prop the melon on the kitchen table
until I return. The orange label reads
Idyll from Marrakech. Ridge lines
of ripeness are beginning to creep
across the brown skin. It is starting
to mellow. I have to be patient.
It will slink into ripeness
like the breasts of a young woman.

Once the plants provided parasols
for snails and mice. I could crawl under
the vines to keep out of the sun.
I touch my forehead and tighten my cap.
I search for an oasis in sand where melons
are grown, avoiding vipers in the dunes.
A trail of vines leads to plumping fruit.
Melons can explode; the sun lights a fuse.

THE SINK STONE

Winter's dirty snow clings
to the north side of the house.
The mailman arrives without good news,
only coupons and catalogs.
Self-pity's clothes don't flatter me.
I walk on white crocuses,
and dim the light of violets
peeping through spikes of grass.

All is happy in this town
and on this street of yawns.
I carry on and raise my arms
as I drown in a pool saluting
the lifeguards and babes
in thongs playing volleyball.

I steal a round rock from
Nobu Restaurant and take it home,
my chopsticks rested on it;
it was so lonely on the counter.
The waiter seems to guess
my wish I were Japanese.

In Rockland, far from Soho,
the stone cries until I place it
on the sink near a yellow
plastic sponge and promise
to get it a companion.

Theft is my true talent.
Next week I will swipe another stone

and place it on top of the first
and bow as I light a candle.
I worship at every shrine I can.
These days are lanterns that swing
for a while and cast no shadows.

BLUE TREES

Ever since you tucked a daisy
in my jacket pocket, I have worn
the flower inside my shirt.

The petals drooped and dried
but never stopped sending signals.
I was alone when I next visited

Purchase, New York. Paintings
and sculpture jammed the galleries
of the Neuberger Museum,

the kiss thrown three years ago
in the mezzanine was lost. Milton Avery
was in soft view, respendent as a goose.

Wandering in his forest of blue trees,
I scratch my way to the surface of a life
tinted dark and inhale the breath of color.

Branches grow in every direction — which
should I climb or hang from?

SNAKESKIN SOUP

I count the torn body bags, black plastic
stuffed with busted pillows, a tired wok, bottles of soy
sauce bleeding last drops, a half eaten pizza.
We make our way from West Houston,
walking on air to downtown alleys off Mulberry.

We stroll down the alleys of Chinatown, her hand
a passport to the Celestial Kingdom — past steaming
noodle shops, the Museum of the Chinese in America,
and elders playing mah-jong in Columbus Park.

She trips down Mott Street with chimes on her ankles;
when she talks, a moon-guitar strums in her throat
yet she is French to her kneecaps, bourgeois as a baguette,
from Paris no less, which forms her special outlook. Beijing
adds color to an aperitif mixed with lapsang tea.

My nose is jade when pressed to jewelers' windows.
A wispy grocer weighs dried snake skins for soup.
We stroll down Lo Mein Alley and a stranger bars her way;
they chatter in Cantonese. I blink, and she's gone.
The sky contracts and buildings sway. . . .

I'm lost in a crowd of Chinese grandmothers
carrying red packages and children. I race through black
alleys and tunnels of light to Bayard Street.
Foreign tourists fill the registers in curio shops.
I sniff like an alley cat confronting a brown rat

and race uptown to sunshine and brownstones. Gargoyles
on the Church on Tenth jeer at me. I lurch
past storefronts in Chelsea; gusts blow in from the river,
prayers from the Jewish cemetery warm my toes.
Winter's cold fingers reach into my pockets. I pass more

cadavers, the broken bones of lovemaking.
The wounded of both sexes beg for dollars,
bearded men with hands out, or tin cups on stumps,
the young, not yet amputees, but already crippled.
Village transvesties wear eyeshadow and lipstick.

I mumble Mozart's Requiem in memory of past
times and happy music. Pedestrians rush
past, faces blurred, gloves gripping briefcases.
I search for her green nap coat bought in Paris.
Transit buses float by like elephants. The bus stop

is mobbed awaiting the next screech of brakes.
Students jump on lugging bottles of Polish water.
Their limbs fold to fit in, no one breathes.
I spin in place holding an overhead strap,
twisting to see everyone. The engine revs, throwing

me off balance. I fall on my face. An old lady smiles.
I collect my knees and look along the rotted piers
and wooden piles rebuilt into tennis courts. Mist creeps
across water. Money squeaks in the pockets of bankers.
The grease of commerce spreads from Wall Street,

like an oil spill that darkens the shores of continents.
Love of power is discernible in black stretch limos,
where you can fuck on the back seat in privacy.
I cricle back to Chinatown like a hungry fish hawk
looking for my love who wore a green coat

and red dress when she disappeared. I pass a funeral
chapel on Doyers Street with ten limos lined up behind
a hearse and open coaches for wreathes and a portrait
of the deceased. I reach over and pick up a large bouquet
and lay it in the hearse as if I were a member

of the family. I shake hands with a weeping son.
We mourn our losses and hug each other.
She's gone and I must bury my memories. A white rose
clings by a thorn to my jacket. The past is glued down
in books upside down and inside out. Her ivory thighs

spoke a world of gestures, her lips spoke Mandarin.
I brush past the bronze sign, "Ng Fook Funerals."
The doors of the limos are closing. There is room for me.
I shake my head, convinced I'm dreaming. On my shoulders,
a casket rides filled with memories.

I kick the tires of the hearse, my head rolls
like a tin can, rebounding onto curbs and hydrants.
I become a stowaway on the ship of Manhattan
and peek out at the horizon from a lifeboat
filled with water. No rainbows curve skyward.

I hide under the Brooklyn Bridge in a brick warehouse,
traffic rumbling above. At midnight, the moon
rises over the latticework and plays tunes
as if the bridge were a giant guitar. I hear her pluck
strings and Parisian melodies resonate.

She flaunts black stockings and her red dress
dances on the cables suspended to Brooklyn.
I hold my breath, afraid she will fall. Instead she
climbs up a gothic tower and yells, "we will meet again in
Chinatown," then dives into darkness.

I search for her like a Mongol sifting sand

with a teaspoon. I'm lost even as I clutch
my worn street map. One way signs point the wrong way.
All of Battery Park is bagged in brown fog.

From Peck Slip, I smell the Fulton Fish Market,
haunt of my father, landmark of my reveries.
The West Side Highway slips into the Hudson.
I inhale the last tugboat on the East River and choke.
The N.Y. Times prints my obit on a blank page.

OLD BRAS

I help my wife find things in a strange city,
her passport, her shoes kicked off in the dark.
The bedroom mirror is in the wrong place
and reflects the wrinkles of our years.
Anniversaries weigh, our tongues sag more.

Nothing fits as well as an old bra,
or if she dares, no bra at all.
My pants are tight and barely zip;
my eyes bulge at the fluid hips
of women with cheeks visibly cleft.

I undress young bodies that flash across
my sight. Berate me! I couldn't care less.
I'm a dirty old man but not dead yet
and hide behind hugs of my grandchildren.
I stretch inside my skin for another look.

DIRTY PICTURES

I cross East Broadway against the light
and the fender of a speeding cab
brushes my coat. I make it to the curb;
the Sikh driver shakes his fist.
Sighing with relief, I buy some falafel
and climb to the roof of a tenement.
I eat slowly and stare down Orchard Street,
pushcarts sprout like trees
and a hundred tongues haggle for life.

I shuffle to Tompkins Square Park,
dizzy, swallowing my thoughts.
The boccie courts are deserted,
a ginkgo leaf falls and touches
my cheek. I'm nauseous
from the odor of sour yesterdays.
White roots and skulls of black settlers
protrude from earth. Beneath the broken
pavement lies a cemetery of blacks
emancipated by death.

Forsythia leap from the shadows
at the sun's command—
what acrobats these plants are!
Warm rain falls on pavements.
Violets open silk umbrellas edging a wet path.
Chinese peonies strangle companions in bed.
I hear coughs of children robed in sweat
sewing coats in a ratty loft.
There are no roses on Essex Street,
geraniums blaze in coffee cans on fire escapes.

I slip on my own shadow crossing
Orchard Street and wake up in Bellevue.
After two hours, I'm released in the custody
of a cockroach. We both look for Katz's deli.
On East Houston we savor the rapture of hot pastrami.
Under a theatre marquee on Second Avenue,
I peddle dirty pictures to tourists — naked senoritas
mounted by donkeys, midgets making love on hat boxes.
Hoarse, I whisper, "two for a nickel, three for a dime."

RED EYES OVER CONGERS

I saw a red fox skulking on the frozen reservoir
as I crossed the causeway. Nose skimming ice,
feet splayed, it was looking for a fat goose or duck
foolish enough to tread water head down
in an open pool.

Even in my car with the heater on, I'm cold. This
is the severest winter in forty years. Ducks remember
the primordial tilt of ice and bite of wind off the west shore.
I'm reminded of glaciers and imagine a new Ice Age
about to descend on Congers, New York.

I have no cows to milk and my chickens roost in the A&P
safe from foxes. Last night I heard the howl of a wolf
and crawled deeper under the blankets. My wife
wondered why I was suddenly romantic. I blamed
the embers from red eyes burning holes in the ice.

BUDAPEST PARK

The trees are bare, the fruit rots
on the ground. Ants invade the cracks
in the shells of fallen chestnuts.

Walking in an orchard of fruit trees
I pick up a rotten apple. Dirt and juice
stain my hands. I find a small russet

pear, my eyes peel the smooth skin
girdling the white flesh the black pits
hide inside. My teeth dive deep

to the core. I'm blessed by the sugar
of ripeness. The theft of fruit satisfies
more than shopping at a market.

Sitting on a park bench I watch
squirrels flounce their tails before flying
up the trunks of trees.

I palm a shiny horse chestnut, rub it
and slip it into my tote bag. A squirrel
steals it when I'm not looking.

PALE LOVERS

She never wore lipstick or perfume
when we met,
no stains on my shirt or jacket,
the footprints of our meeting
in Tribeca were air and clouds,
we never held hands in public,
the hydrants had eyes,
the turnips gossiped.
When climbing mountains in Chinatown,
an avalanche of feeling.
I was trapped.

DRUMS OF INDIAN SUMMER

Skunk spray from a distance
tickles my nose. The wind rolls down
Hi Tor mussing my hair. Deer flies
fill up with blood from my arm.

I doze as winesaps ripen. The sounds
from Davies Farm are muffled, cider
barrels are being cleaned. Families
pay to harvest McCouns and Macs.

The slate-grey swells of Lake DeForest
churn in my mind. Fall will arrive
with a new paint job. Apple pickers
sing in Spanish leaning from ladders.

Unsinkable geese land and pound
the water. I have never hunted
fowl, only fish in and out of season.
If carp could fly, I would shoot them.

I rest my toes in the bottom
of a leaking row boat. The oars
no longer slice water but rest on lilies.
The grief of sleep is in the waking.

FLOWERS FROM THE DOGHOUSE

I buy flowers for my wife
on Fridays, usually
I like their color and smell
but can't remember their names.
Mrs. Scheu, the florist, always
tells me but I forget.

I walk them home on a leash
and they stop at every hydrant
and sniff. When no one watches,
they drizzle on red metal and whine.
These blooms tug when we cross
Lake Road afraid of being run over.

A POLISH OUTHOUSE IN BROOKLYN

Father built an outhouse from memory
in Brooklyn with a peaked roof like in Poland.
His sister also wanted a henhouse. He nailed it
together in a weekend. The hens clucked
in Polish, the rooster crowed in Russian.

There was peace in America.
Brown eggs rolled into the kitchen
where my Tante Kaille baked challah.
Horses pulled milkwagons, not cannon.
I ran along and trotted with the horses.

SKUNK CABBAGE

Blades of grass lie folded, uncut
since Thanksgiving. The necklace
of ice around the lake still sparkles.

I walk carefully, the ground
squishes water. My wife and son
disappear below the horizon of
my childhood as skunk cabbage parade
in swamps below the town dump.

Harry Waitzman is a retired judge living in Congers, New York. He was raised on a farm in Rockland County where he played in streams overgrown with skunk cabbage. As a teenager he enlisted in the U.S. Navy serving as a crew chief. He attended the University of Pennsylvania and Columbia Law School and worked as a country lawyer and town judge. He decided poetry was the most important thing in his life, went to Sarah Lawrence College and graduated with an M.F.A. in 1993. His chapbook, "Seven Views of Hudson's River," was published in 1987. He is published widely in literary journals. He and his wife Marcia have two children and five grandchildren. He is at work on a second collection of poems.

Mudfish Individual Poet Series

No. 1: David Lawrence, *Dementia Pugilistica*

No. 2: Jill Hoffman, *Black Diaries*

No. 3: Doug Dorph, *Too Too Flesh*

No. 4: Harry Waitzman, *Skunk Cabbage*

Box Turtle Press
184 Franklin Street
New York, New York 10013
212.219.9278
Mudfishmag@aol.com